D1530154

More Feelings Only I Know

Fighting...
How It Makes
Me Feel

Funny Feelings Aren't
Really Funny!

Feeling Important
Is Important!

... establishes a comfortable means for conversation and expression by children, while fostering understanding of divorce. Reading this book is a vital step in rebuilding a broken family. It provides a healthy way for children to deal with divorce before it can be stored away as baggage that is carried around for life. By utilizing this book, parents will also be touched emotionally and can learn to change *their* behavior — whether they read it with their children, or read it themselves out of curiosity.

Written by Susan McKenna
Illustrated by Shelley Johannes

Wayfarer Press, LLC

Published by:
Wayfarer Press, LLC
PO Box 948
Union Lake, Michigan, 48387-0948
www.wayfarerbooks.com
wayfarerpress@sbcglobal.net

ISBN-13: 978-0-9789965-1-2
ISBN-10: 0-9789965-1-8

Library of Congress Control Number: 2007931214

Illustrations: Shelley Johannes

Printed in Korea

First Edition

FOREWORD

Wayne County's Family Court handles over 20,000 divorces and child-custody cases each year. As a Circuit Court Judge for seven years and Family Law Counselor for 10 years, I have seen firsthand the devastation and damage to children of divorce. They overwhelmingly internalize the blame and responsibility for the parental relationship and subsequent breakup. Continuing conflict between parents not only reinforces this mistaken belief, but can also cause irreparable harm.

Susan McKenna's *More Feelings Only I Know* helps parents intentionally create a scenario for children where positive relationships are the expected norm. It also helps parents to get beyond their own hurt and anger by re-committing themselves to placing the psychological welfare of their children first.

As a divorced mother myself, I have personally observed and worked through the emotional turmoil and stress experienced by children during this difficult time. I highly recommend the suggestions presented in *More Feelings Only I Know*. They are psychologically solid and, if followed, will go a long way in creating a more positive and healthy experience for children.

Honorable Kathleen M. McCarthy
Wayne County Circuit Court – Family Division

Fighting...
How It Makes
Me Feel

When mom and dad
fight with each other,
          kids like me feel scared.

It feels like they are really hurting each other.
Sometimes, mom and dad sound mean to each other.
          Sometimes, they are crying.

          It makes me hurt inside.
               Inside of me, where they cannot see,
                    it feels really bad.

3

I want to do something.
I want to make mom and dad
stop fighting.

I want to do something
        so I cannot hear them.

I want the fighting to go away
        and never, ever
                come back!

4

Please don't fight so I can hear you...
it hurts my heart!

It hurts me to see you making each other
feel bad, especially when it's
another person I love.

It scares me to see you like this.
You are supposed to make *me*
feel safe.

I do not want to know
what you are fighting about,
and I don't want to hear you hurting.

Maybe mom and dad
just need to hear me.

They need to know
how my heart feels when they fight.

It will make me feel better
if I tell them how I feel.

6

After I tell mom and dad how I feel
in my heart, maybe they will need a big, fat hug.
A hug that lasts a long time —
those are the best!

Giving hugs
and telling someone
you love how
you feel is the
right thing
to do!

7

Funny Feelings Aren't Really Funny!

When I get in trouble for something I did, usually I know I did something wrong.

8

Lately, I get in trouble when I really don't know what I have done wrong.

Sometimes, I feel like everything I do makes mom or dad angry.

At other times, I feel like mom and dad don't even know I am here.
      I don't feel very important…

I might do something wrong
just so mom and dad pay attention to me.

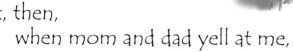

But, then,
when mom and dad yell at me,
it doesn't make me feel
like they love me.

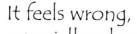

It feels wrong,
especially when they yell at me a lot.
Sometimes, my mom and dad don't even notice when I try to be good,
or when I try to make them happy.

Sometimes, they yell when I make mistakes.

If mom and dad
would tell me what I did
to make them angry, maybe I could fix it.

If I could fix it, I would be much happier.

But sometimes I cannot fix it.
Sometimes, I cannot make it better.

1 1

When mom and dad yell at me,
I feel bad because I feel like I made them sad.

It is not my fault they are fighting.
It is not my fault they are getting a divorce.

It is not my fault when they are not
having a good day.

I NEED TO FEEL THE THINGS I DO
MAKE THEM PROUD OF ME.

I want to know mom is happy,

and I want to know dad is happy.

I want to hear about the things I do right.
I need to hear about the things I do that help you feel good.
Helping others feel good makes me feel good.

What can I do to help mom and dad feel good?

14

Feeling Important Is Important!

When mom and dad get busy,
they have to fit a lot of things into the day.

Lately, mom and dad have had a lot of things to do.
They are very busy, but they still love me!

15

Some days, though, I feel alone. Sometimes, I feel like I am invisible.

Sometimes, I feel like hiding behind a chair so they will come find me.

When mom or dad is busy, or have other things to do, it keeps them from spending time with me. It is not much fun.

Maybe I can share fun things,
special things that make me feel happy.

I can share the things that make me feel special and important.

17

I like feeling important.
I know that other things are important, too, but so am I.

Sometimes, it helps mom and dad if I remind them
that I miss doing stuff with them.
I like when they spend time with me.

I will be able to spend special time
with mom…

And then, sometimes, I will
spend special time with dad.

That will be very nice.

A special time could be bedtime.
I can share hugs and cuddle.
I can talk about funny things.

We can laugh and be silly.

Maybe it will be fun to help make dinner.
We can eat our dinner on a big blanket on the floor,
and pretend it's a picnic.
That would be fun, even if we are indoors.

I like spending time doing fun
things with each of them.

Fun times make me smile.

20

When I have a fun time with mom,
dad is happy.

When I spend fun time with dad,
mom is happy.

Pretty soon, we will all be happy,
all at the same time!

(Put a happy picture of you here.)

I ♡ MY FAMILY

22

Special Parental Guide

NOTE: *If you and your children have not already read the first book in this series,* Feelings Only I Know, *you may want to consider doing so. While either book may be read as a stand-alone aid, the first book provides a good introduction for children when dealing with divorce.*

A recurring theme in almost every class and every divorce support group is the issue of fighting between divorcing/divorced parents. The problem, of course, is that children don't understand such bitterness between mom and dad, and that confuses and frustrates them. It also makes the children feel unimportant at a time when they most need to feel important.

Now, in reality, it is impossible to ask two adults going through a breakup not to argue. However, for the sake of your children, it is important to choose *where, when* and *how* you argue or fight. Above all, do NOT fight with the children present, or within earshot. This also means not discussing and reliving your spousal arguments with friends and family where your children can hear. While *you* may need sympathetic ears on which to vent, or simply update others on what is going on, this can have a very negative impact on your children. As mentioned above, it confuses, frustrates and frightens them. It can also add to their insecurities and doubts about the future, which is even worse. Your children need to feel safe, and seeing mom and dad fight — even after a divorce — does not accomplish this at all.

That's because fighting between adults is an *adult* issue, and young children simply do not have the skills to interpret such behavior or to handle it at their age. As an adult, *you* probably can't make sense of your breakup, nor can you decide what to do. It makes you furious and frustrated, and you are an *adult*. What do you think your arguing/fighting with your ex (or soon-to-be ex) is doing to your children?

By exposing them to fighting, along with the words and emotions expressed in the arguments, your children will not only be bothered at the moment, they will continue to relive the negative words and feelings they experience. This can ultimately manifest as stress, anxiety, fear, hurt, and doubt every time they think or dream about it. It will affect them daily.

Remember, there is a time and place for everything. As far as you're concerned, *you* probably need a break from fighting, too. Even when not fighting with your partner, divorcing adults seem to rehash the fights with anyone who will listen. Again, take a break, for your own good. Living in such an atmosphere is not good for anyone, and not good for a family that needs healing, first and foremost. Go on a fighting "diet" and limit your exposure to it.

And if you say, "It is my spouse who always starts the fights," keep in mind that YOU can still exercise control over the situation. It takes *two* to fight. If it occurs on the phone, you have the option of ending the call. If you fight when you see each other, avoid seeing each other, if possible, or enlist a friend or family member to be there when the kids are picked up, or have someone else drop them off, etc.

When you and your ex lived together, it was different. If you're already divorced and no longer live together, you can control when/how you see your ex, so make wise choices, for the sake of your children. "Baggage," as we adults call it, can be a result of unaddressed issues from childhood, so don't just sweep them under the carpet or underestimate the emotional havoc they may be causing your family.

Exercise/Activity

When you sense your children are struggling after an especially trying time/event, this exercise is designed to help them "get it out," rather than bottling up negative emotions. You'll need some crayons, or pencils/markers, and paper. Perhaps, you could buy a journal so children can have a special book for this activity. Then keep it in a special place, like a special box under their bed or in a closet. You might even encourage your children to draw on the outside of the box to see where your children's emotions take them (angry faces on the box, for example).

Thus, when your children feel bad, they can get out their "angry box" and draw pictures of what they're feeling in their journal, returning the book to the box and the box to its hiding place when done. Tell them if they want to share the pictures with you, they can…and that you will *not* get angry or judge them. Or, they may choose *not* to show you, and you agree not to peek. Emphasize that it is *their* box. If they *do* show you what they wrote or drew, try not to be judgmental or defensive. Remember, we all say things in anger because we can't hold emotions inside; and that's the *purpose* of this therapeutic activity for your children: *to get the negative emotions out.*

If any issues do arise that need to be discussed, discuss as appropriate and offer affirming, reassuring statements, such as: "I can see how you might feel like that." Or, "I am sorry I/we made you feel like that."

Finally, take a vow that you will keep whatever your children share with you in confidence and never use it against your ex. This activity is between you and your children, so do not destroy their confidence in your private relationship. (**NOTE**: Be sure to consult your attorney, however, for any legal responsibilities you may have in the case of serious abuse, should you discover it.)

And, remember, as in the first book, *Feelings Only I Know,* this book has been illustrated with hidden hearts on each page for you and your children to find together. It's also a reminder to your children, and you, *of the love and the good things that you both still have, even during the difficulties of divorce.*

FEELINGS

Also keep in mind that your children's feelings aren't right or wrong. They are what they are and are true for the person who's feeling them. They are also very real for young children and need to be taken seriously by parents. If your children don't feel important, or don't sense that you're taking their feelings seriously, words alone won't change that. Children understand and gauge their importance by the quality time you devote to them and their needs and issues.

Kids, especially during divorce, need *you*. Not you with a new friend, not you while you are juggling every crisis that occurs in the day, and not you listening while doing something else. Children need special time just with you, especially when trying to recover and heal. So, put it on your calendar and set quality time aside. Make it a daily ritual, even if it is only for short periods each day.

It may surprise you, but children are also very aware that *you* are hurting, even if you are putting on a brave face. And, your children probably want desperately to do something to make you feel better. You can help them "help you" by sharing and caring together, by explaining that people do things for others just to make them smile, or lessen a burden, or simply to make their day better.

Then, discuss some things your children can do that will make your day better, and then take the time to acknowledge it and reciprocate. They could help you water the plants, read you a book, take a walk with you, help you fold laundry. Even such little things can mean a lot. When they do it, take the time to enjoy the fact that someone loves you as much as they do. Sometimes, divorcing adults focus so much on the love they have lost that they forget to celebrate *the love they still have*. Through divorce, however, you can learn to appreciate the people who do love you more than ever.

FEELING IMPORTANT

Feeling important is something that every person appreciates, including your children. And both parents need to participate. To do so, be sure to facilitate a healthy relationship with the other parent if at all possible, regardless of your personal feelings. Just because your ex wasn't a good spouse, doesn't mean they should be a bad parent. Although some people find validation in a spouse showing his/her true colors by not being the parent they should be, your children are the ones who will suffer tremendously by the lack of this parent in their life.

Even though your marriage may be over, your job as parents is not. It is much better for your children if both parents can make this a coordinated effort. Children need to see both parents interested in school and activities whenever possible. However, don't be too harsh on the other parent if that person can't be at *every* function. Married couples cannot always attend every function, so it is no different when you are divorced.

If you can stop worrying about what the other parent is or is not doing and spend that energy on *your* actions, your children will benefit. It is hard not to judge the other parent when you see that their actions affect your children. But that is when *your* actions need to become even more special. Consider it an opportunity — not to crush your ex — but to be there for your hurting children. Listen to what *they* are feeling and reassure them that the other parent cares for them, too. Do what *you* have to do to make your children feel that they have TWO parents that love them.

Even though it feels good to be the better parent, your children will never be happy or feel complete by having one of the two of you absent from their life. Some parents make it difficult for their ex to stay active with their children because they are trying to punish the ex for leaving or ending the marriage. However, nothing can replace an absent parent. Your children will benefit from having both parents in their life, even if one is not as responsible or available as the other. Take what you can get and try to facilitate an atmosphere that welcomes whatever that parent can provide, and know the good it is doing for your children.

The greatest gift you can give your children is to be a happy and healthy parent…*both* parents. Do what you have to do to be that person. Therapy, self improvement, regaining a spiritual connection…do whatever it takes and provide a happy, safe and nurturing environment for you and your children. Each school system has a social worker available to help your children at no cost. Therapy may also be available at no cost if you do not have insurance. Churches also offer divorce recovery for children and adults, so check with your church, or for resources on the Internet.

There are many resources available for divorced parents, so don't be afraid to seek them out. Your local library can also be of great help, as there are numerous books, DVDs and videos available on these subjects. The more information you have, the more good things can come out of your situation.

You can either be a victim or a victor. Grow through your divorce and make your family stronger in spite of it.